Super Cowgirl and Mighty Miracle

By

JOSÉ CRUZ GONZÁLEZ

Dramatic Publishing Company
Woodstock, Illinois ● Australia ● New Zealand ● South Africa

IMPORTANT BILLING AND CREDIT REQUIREMENTS

All producers of the play *must* give credit to the author of the play in all programs distributed in connection with performances of the play and in all instances in which the title of the play appears for purposes of advertising, publicizing or otherwise exploiting the play and/or a production. The name of the author *must* also appear on a separate line, on which no other name appears, immediately following the title, and *must* appear in size of type not less than fifty percent (50%) the size of the title type. Biographical information on the author, if included in the playbook, may be used in all programs. *In all programs this notice must appear:*

"Produced by special arrangement with
THE DRAMATIC PUBLISHING COMPANY, INC., of Woodstock, Illinois."

For Penny

Super Cowgirl and Mighty Miracle was commissioned and developed by Metro Theater Company and premiered on Sept. 27, 2011, touring to Zion Lutheran School in Belleville, Ill.

Director .... Carol North
Stage Manager ....Sarah Rugo
Costume Design...Lou Bird
Sound Design.. Rusty Wandall
Set Design .... Nicholas Kryah

Cast:
Nicholas Kryah ....Dog/Miracle
Peggy Neely-Harris............................. Grandmother Autumn
Leah Stewart .... Cory

The play was first developed at Metro Theater Company's New Work Incubator in December 2009 and October 2010 as part of The American Arts Experience—St. Louis. It was also workshopped at NYU's 13th Annual New Plays for Young Audiences in June 2010.

Super Cowgirl and Mighty Miracle received a second production and tour at Childsplay on March 22-30, 2014 at the Tempe Center for the Arts. The cast included Chanel Bragg, Osiris Cuen, Carlos A. Lara and Jon Gentry. Kish Finnegan, costume design; Joey Trahan, sound design; Douglas Clarke, scenic design; Joel Thompson, lighting design; D. Daniel Hollingshead, hair & makeup design. Ellen Beckett, stage manager. Dwayne Hartford, director.

Special thanks to
Emily Kohring, Nancy Swortzell, Cecily O'Neill,
NYU, the Metro Theater Company community and
Our Lady of Guadalupe School in St. Louis.

Super Cowgirl and Mighty Miracle

CHARACTERS

CORY: a 6-year-old girl of mixed heritage, Latina/African-American. Bright, curious, wild imagination, loves to read and invent games.

GRANDMOTHER AUTUMN: a middle-aged African-American woman with a toothache. College educated and unemployed. On the verge of losing her home. A church lady who loves to wear her hat to church. Regal, stern, independent and set in her ways. Widowed.

DOG/MIRACLE: a homeless dog with an unstoppable life force. Playful, happy, loving, nurturing, loves to run, chase things, chew stuff, eat and sleep on his back.

TIME & PLACE

2011. A neighborhood where wild dandelions grow and foreclosure signs flourish.

Super Cowgirl and Mighty Miracle

(GRANDMOTHER AUTUMN and CORY stand onstage. CORY wears a jacket, cowboy boots and a cowboy hat. She carries a backpack and holds onto a toy dog named Bandit.)

GRANDMOTHER AUTUMN *(to CORY's unseen father)*. You want to leave your daughter with me?

CORY *(to her unseen father)*. *Papi*, I don't want to stay with her!

GRANDMOTHER AUTUMN. After everything we've gone through?

CORY. I don't care if she's my mommy's mommy!

GRANDMOTHER AUTUMN. You took my Sara away and now she's gone.

CORY. Her house is scary!

GRANDMOTHER AUTUMN. Don't make any promises you can't keep.

CORY. I'll stay in the truck and I won't whine!

GRANDMOTHER AUTUMN. I don't want her.

CORY. I want you!

GRANDMOTHER AUTUMN. What job?

CORY. Why can't I go?

GRANDMOTHER AUTUMN. I'm looking for work, too.

CORY. What city?

GRANDMOTHER AUTUMN. I burned through my savings.

CORY. Please take me with you!

GRANDMOTHER AUTUMN. I don't even have health insurance.

CORY. Please, *Papi*!

GRANDMOTHER AUTUMN. You're sleeping in a truck?

CORY. I won't be a crybaby!

GRANDMOTHER AUTUMN. What kind of father are you?

CORY. I'll be a good girl!

GRANDMOTHER AUTUMN. Fine, she can stay, but it's only temporary.

CORY. No!

GRANDMOTHER AUTUMN. There's the front gate.

CORY. Don't go!

GRANDMOTHER AUTUMN. Go!

CORY. *¡PAPI!*

(A truck is heard driving away.)

GRANDMOTHER AUTUMN. Lord, what now? *(To CORY.)* There's no need for tears. It's cold. Let's go inside.

(CORY doesn't move.)

GRANDMOTHER AUTUMN *(cont'd)*. You can't stay out here by yourself. That's my first rule. There're vicious dogs running around the neighborhood. They're wild and hungry. I'll make supper.

(In the kitchen. They sit. GRANDMOTHER AUTUMN serves CORY a bowl of soup. CORY smells it and makes a face.)

GRANDMOTHER AUTUMN *(cont'd)*. Baby, you gotta eat your soup.

CORY. I'm no baby. My name is Cory. Cory *Angelica Torres*.

GRANDMOTHER AUTUMN. Torres?

CORY. *Torres.*

GRANDMOTHER AUTUMN. OK, Cory *Angelicaaa Torres*! You gotta eat your soup.

CORY. No.

GRANDMOTHER AUTUMN. I made it fresh for you.

CORY. It came out of a can I saw.

GRANDMOTHER AUTUMN. OK, you're right. You wanna grow up to be big and strong, don't you? That's why you gotta eat your chicken soup.

CORY. I don't like chicken soup. Chicken soup comes from chicken poop.

GRANDMOTHER AUTUMN. What?

CORY. They poop in everything especially soup.

GRANDMOTHER AUTUMN. That's nonsense.

CORY *(pointing into the bowl)*. What's that?

GRANDMOTHER AUTUMN. That's chicken meat.

CORY. Poop.

GRANDMOTHER AUTUMN. No.

CORY. What's that?

GRANDMOTHER AUTUMN. Noodles.

CORY. Big poop.

GRANDMOTHER AUTUMN. Child, where did you learn this?

CORY. Madeleine Perry-Chang told me.

GRANDMOTHER AUTUMN. Who's she?

CORY. My study buddy.

GRANDMOTHER AUTUMN. You believe her?

CORY. Yup, ah huh, she's the smartest kid in first grade.

GRANDMOTHER AUTUMN. Well, she's wrong.

CORY. How do you know?

GRANDMOTHER AUTUMN. 'Cause I went to college. So who's smarter now? Eat your soup.

(CORY refuses. She crosses her arms.)

GRANDMOTHER AUTUMN *(cont'd)*. Food costs money. I count every penny. Second rule. "What Grandma Autumn serves, you'll eat or you'll sit there all night."

(GRANDMOTHER AUTUMN crosses her arms.)

CORY. Poop.

GRANDMOTHER AUTUMN. Soup.

CORY. Poop.

GRANDMOTHER AUTUMN. Soup.

CORY. Poop.

GRANDMOTHER AUTUMN. OK, time for bed!

CORY. But I'm not sleepy.

GRANDMOTHER AUTUMN. Well, I am. I'm older than you.

(They prepare a place for CORY to sleep.)

GRANDMOTHER AUTUMN *(cont'd)*. Now lie down.

CORY. My daddy reads to me before I sleep.

GRANDMOTHER AUTUMN. I can't picture that.

CORY. He's a real good reader. The best.

GRANDMOTHER AUTUMN. Fine.

(CORY hands GRANDMOTHER AUTUMN a book.)

GRANDMOTHER AUTUMN *(cont'd)*. *Forever Poppy.* *"When—"*

CORY. —Forever *Flor* Keyshawn *Isla*-Baptiste-Poppy was born—

GRANDMOTHER AUTUMN. "—her parents believed in honoring their ancestors—"

CORY. —by giving her a very long and complicated name.

GRANDMOTHER AUTUMN. "So Forever *Flor* Keyshawn *Isla*-Baptiste-Poppy—"

CORY. —was just known as Forever Poppy.

GRANDMOTHER AUTUMN. Why am I reading to you if you all ready memorized the book?

CORY. 'Cause it's my favorite in the whole world.

GRANDMOTHER AUTUMN. Maybe I should read you something else.

CORY. That's all I got. *Papi* had to sell everything. All my things fit in here. *(She holds up her backpack.)*

GRANDMOTHER AUTUMN. Well, this is all I got: four walls, a bedroom, kitchen and bathroom.

CORY. It's more than I got.

GRANDMOTHER AUTUMN. Well, then we agree on something.

CORY *(points)*. What's that?

GRANDMOTHER AUTUMN. It's my church hat. You're not allowed to touch it. That's rule number three. Now, lie down and close your eyes.

CORY. I can't.

GRANDMOTHER AUTUMN. Why not?

CORY. The sofa bed creaks.

GRANDMOTHER AUTUMN. Well, that's 'cause it's old.

CORY. Something's outside my window.

GRANDMOTHER AUTUMN. It's a tree's shadow caused by the moonlight.

CORY. You got monsters under here?

GRANDMOTHER AUTUMN. Monsters? There's no such thing as monsters.

CORY. Yes, there is.

GRANDMOTHER AUTUMN. Well, they don't come near this house.

CORY. Why not?

GRANDMOTHER AUTUMN. 'Cause they're scared of me.

CORY. Why?

GRANDMOTHER AUTUMN. I deep fry them in oil and eat them with Tabasco sauce!

CORY. *¡PAPI!*

GRANDMOTHER AUTUMN. It's a joke! I'm kidding! If there were monsters, they wouldn't come to my house 'cause I eat chicken soup. That's what really keeps them away.

CORY. Can I sleep in your bed?

GRANDMOTHER AUTUMN. You're a big girl. You've got your own space. I'll leave the light on.

CORY. Please don't close the door.

GRANDMOTHER AUTUMN. OK. Good night.

CORY. Night.

(GRANDMOTHER AUTUMN exits. CORY sits up. She peeks over the edge of the sofa bed.)

CORY *(cont'd, timidly)*. Is anybody there?

GRANDMOTHER AUTUMN *(offstage)*. Go to sleep!

(CORY throws the blanket over her. The next morning. Music. GRANDMOTHER AUTUMN enters gently brushing her teeth. She stands before an imaginary sink and mirror. CORY gets up and brushes her teeth before an imaginary sink and mirror. They go through their morning ritual unaware what the other is doing. GRANDMOTHER AUTUMN puts on her church hat. CORY puts on her cowboy hat.)

CORY. Yeehaw, Super Cowgirl!

GRANDMOTHER AUTUMN. You can't wear that in church.

CORY. Why not?

GRANDMOTHER AUTUMN. 'Cause the Lord's house isn't the "Wild West."

CORY. The Lord should let cowgirls into church.

GRANDMOTHER AUTUMN. Well, you'll just have to take that up with him.

(GRANDMOTHER AUTUMN takes the cowboy hat off CORY.)

GRANDMOTHER AUTUMN *(cont'd)*. We're going to church, then the food bank, and come home.

CORY. Why do we got to go to church?

GRANDMOTHER AUTUMN. Your parents never took you to church?

CORY. Nope. We went for waffles, instead!

GRANDMOTHER AUTUMN. Oh, Lord!

(A church bell is heard. GRANDMOTHER AUTUMN carries an umbrella.)

CORY. Is it gonna rain?

GRANDMOTHER AUTUMN. No. It's to protect us from those wild dogs.

CORY. Why are they wild?

GRANDMOTHER AUTUMN. 'Cause the neighbors left them behind when they moved out.

CORY. There's nobody to love them?

GRANDMOTHER AUTUMN. There's nothing to love about them. They're nasty and they'll bite your head off. Now stay close. *(A car passes by, sending out a friendly honk.)* Good morning, Mr. Johnson!

CORY. Look at all those pretty flowers!

GRANDMOTHER AUTUMN. They're dandelions, unwanted weeds.

CORY. Can I pick some?

GRANDMOTHER AUTUMN. No, you can't.

CORY. But there's so many of them.

GRANDMOTHER AUTUMN. You see all them for sale signs? Most of my neighbors moved out 'cause they've been robbed of their homes.

CORY. How'd their homes get robbed?

GRANDMOTHER AUTUMN. By those no-good-for-nothing thieves in fancy suits and ties wearing expensive shoes and cologne on Wall Street. They're the ones that caused this mess. You borrow money from them and they'll choke the life out of you.

CORY. Their mommies or daddies should talk to them about being bad.

GRANDMOTHER AUTUMN. Take their privileges away!

CORY. Put them in time out!

GRANDMOTHER AUTUMN. Put them in jail!

CORY. No TV!

GRANDMOTHER AUTUMN. No parole!

(DOG enters. He carries an old belt with a shiny buckle in his mouth. He looks lost.)

CORY. Look, it's a doggy!

GRANDMOTHER AUTUMN. Don't go near him.

CORY. He looks friendly.

GRANDMOTHER AUTUMN. He might bite you.

CORY. He's got a belt in his mouth.

GRANDMOTHER AUTUMN. That's 'cause he's crazy. Shoo!

CORY. Poor doggy.

(CORY crosses to DOG. He drops the belt in front of her. He looks at her, then the belt, back to her, then the belt. He nudges her. She picks it up and pets him.)

CORY *(cont'd)*. Can we keep him?

GRANDMOTHER AUTUMN. What? No!

CORY. I promise I'll feed him!

GRANDMOTHER AUTUMN. I can't afford to raise you and a dog!

CORY. I'll play with him everyday!

GRANDMOTHER AUTUMN. He's dirty and carries diseases!

CORY. Please!

GRANDMOTHER AUTUMN. I said, "No!" *(To DOG.)* GO AWAY! *(Lifting her umbrella as if to strike him. He yelps and runs away. To CORY.)* Hurry now! Let's go before he follows us!

(Church music.)

GRANDMOTHER AUTUMN *(cont'd, to the unseen church ladies)*. Good morning, Sister Edwina! What a beautiful new hat you have. My, they charged you that much? Sister Hattie, so very nice to see you! What an elegant hat you're wearing! Oh, it's from Atlanta? Sister Esther, I love the plumage! You look like a peacock! Praise the Lord.

CORY. Their hats are bigger than yours.

GRANDMOTHER AUTUMN *(to CORY)*. Shhh! *(To the unseen church ladies.)* Who's this? It's my granddaughter Cory. Say hello to the nice ladies, Cory.

CORY. Hello.

GRANDMOTHER AUTUMN. They don't get to visit me much. I always have to go to them.

CORY. Huh?

GRANDMOTHER AUTUMN. Close your mouth, dear. It's not polite. *(To the unseen church ladies.)* Kids, today! *(Music is heard.)* Ladies. *(To CORY.)* Sit down.

CORY. You lied.

GRANDMOTHER AUTUMN. No, I didn't.

CORY. Broke the truth.

GRANDMOTHER AUTUMN. No, I bent it a little that's all.

CORY. I don't remember you ever coming to visit us.

GRANDMOTHER AUTUMN. That's 'cause you were a baby in diapers. All you could do is eat and sleep.

CORY. Can we go now?

GRANDMOTHER AUTUMN. No, service just started.

CORY. But I can't see anything.

GRANDMOTHER AUTUMN. Don't embarrass me in front of these ladies.

CORY. Can I have some gum?

GRANDMOTHER AUTUMN. No!

(Church music begins. GRANDMOTHER AUTUMN stands and pulls CORY up, too. DOG walks in carrying a large feather in his mouth. He crosses to CORY dropping it in front of her.)

CORY. Hey, is this for me? How did you find me? Have you come to pray? Don't let Grandma see you!

(CORY pets him. DOG stands behind GRANDMOTHER AUTUMN and CORY. A woman's voice is heard screaming, "Lord, almighty!")

GRANDMOTHER AUTUMN *(to DOG)*. You! *(To congregation.)* He's not my dog! I've never seen him before!

(DOG yelps and runs off. Chaos ensues in church.)

GRANDMOTHER AUTUMN *(taking CORY by the hand)*. Let's go!

(At the church food bank.)

CORY. I'm hungry.

GRANDMOTHER AUTUMN. So am I.

CORY. We've been waiting in line forever.

GRANDMOTHER AUTUMN. Look, the food bank is open now. *(Beat. To the unseen church ladies.)* Sister Edwina, Esther and Hattie? What a surprise to see you. No, I didn't come to volunteer today.

CORY. SpaghettiOs!

GRANDMOTHER AUTUMN. Don't be rude, Cory. We'll take whatever the good ladies give us. I'm here for her.

(A bus is heard. GRANDMOTHER AUTUMN and CORY ride a bus. GRANDMOTHER AUTUMN carries a bag filled with groceries.)

CORY. Are we there yet?

GRANDMOTHER AUTUMN. We're not far.

CORY. I'm tired.

GRANDMOTHER AUTUMN. I'll make us lunch when we get home.

CORY. I hope it's not chicken soup.

GRANDMOTHER AUTUMN. They gave us baloney, bread, milk, bananas and yes, more chicken soup. You should be grateful for what we've been given.

CORY. Why do you always do that?

GRANDMOTHER AUTUMN. Do what?

CORY. Look like you're mad.

GRANDMOTHER AUTUMN. I've got a toothache.

CORY. Why can't you fix it?

GRANDMOTHER AUTUMN. When I get a job I will. Until then I'm just going to look mad.

(The bus stops. They get off. The bus drives away.)

CORY. We're home.

GRANDMOTHER AUTUMN. Stay in the yard. I'm getting yesterday's mail.

CORY. Yes, ma'am.

GRANDMOTHER AUTUMN. Remember now, keep that gate closed.

(GRANDMOTHER AUTUMN goes to get her mail. Dogs are heard.)

CORY. Grandma!

GRANDMOTHER AUTUMN. Shoo! Shoo!

(Dogs charge after the grocery bag.)

CORY. Grandma!

GRANDMOTHER AUTUMN. Stay in the yard! *(She beats the dogs with her umbrella. Catching her breath.)* I'm fine. I'm fine.

CORY. Is it a letter from my *papi*?

GRANDMOTHER AUTUMN. I don't think—

CORY. He likes to draw pictures. Let's open it!

GRANDMOTHER AUTUMN. Child, it's not from your daddy, it's from the bank.

(DOG enters carrying a colorful piece of ribbon in his mouth.)

CORY. Hey— *(DOG drops the ribbon in front of CORY.)* Hello, boy! *(DOG barks.)*

GRANDMOTHER AUTUMN. No!

(GRANDMOTHER AUTUMN hits him with her umbrella. DOG yelps running off. CORY starts to cry.)

CORY. You hurt him! *Papi* said you were nice, but you're not! You're mean!

GRANDMOTHER AUTUMN. Watch your mouth, child!

CORY. I want my *papi*!

GRANDMOTHER AUTUMN. He's not here! It's just me!

CORY. I hate you!

GRANDMOTHER AUTUMN. I hate my life!

CORY. *Papi*!!!

(CORY runs off.)

GRANDMOTHER AUTUMN. Cory, come back here! Cory!

(GRANDMOTHER AUTUMN chases after her. CORY re-enters. She realizes she's lost.)

CORY. Grandma?

(DOG enters carrying rhinestone trim in his mouth. He crosses to CORY dropping it in front of her.)

CORY *(cont't)*. It's you again! *(She hugs DOG.)* Why do you keep bringing me things?

(GRANDMOTHER AUTUMN enters catching her breath.)

CORY *(cont'd)*. I'm sorry Grandma scared you. She scares me. She don't like us.

(DOG senses GRANDMOTHER AUTUMN. They turn to her.)

GRANDMOTHER AUTUMN *(to CORY)*. Please don't do that again.

CORY. Grandma?

GRANDMOTHER AUTUMN. Now, let's go home.

CORY. No. You hit him. That was so mean.

GRANDMOTHER AUTUMN. Well, I'm sorry. Come on.

CORY. No, there's nobody to play with, and why can't I play outside?

GRANDMOTHER AUTUMN. OK, you can play in the front yard as long as you keep the gate closed.

CORY. Can he come, too?

GRANDMOTHER AUTUMN. Do you promise not to run away?

(CORY nods her head "yes.")

CORY. Does that mean I get to keep him?

GRANDMOTHER AUTUMN. I make no promises. We'll take it one day at a time.

CORY *(to DOG)*. Where's your family, boy? Are you hungry? I think he's hungry. I'm hungry.

GRANDMOTHER AUTUMN. Me, too.

(She holds out her hand to CORY. CORY takes it. They exit. DOG follows. The front yard. DOG enters and circles the yard. He pauses momentarily and resumes his play. GRANDMOTHER AUTUMN and CORY soon follow.)

GRANDMOTHER AUTUMN. That dog sleeps outside.

CORY. Can't he sleep with me?

GRANDMOTHER AUTUMN. No.

CORY. He's going to be scared at night.

GRANDMOTHER AUTUMN. He's a dog, not a human.

CORY. He's got feelings.

GRANDMOTHER AUTUMN. No, he doesn't.

CORY. Madeleine Perry-Chang says—

GRANDMOTHER AUTUMN. Who went to college?

CORY. You did.

GRANDMOTHER AUTUMN *(sniffing)*. What's that awful smell?

CORY. Poop. You stepped in it.

(GRANDMOTHER AUTUMN groans and scrapes her foot on the ground next to the rose bush.)

GRANDMOTHER AUTUMN *(cont'd)*. Make sure that mutt stays away from my rose plant.

CORY. What rose plant?

GRANDMOTHER AUTUMN *(pointing to a plastic garbage bag)*. This one.

CORY. Why do you got plastic on it?

GRANDMOTHER AUTUMN. To keep the cold out and the warmth in.

(GRANDMOTHER AUTUMN removes the plastic bag revealing a shoot in a flower pot.)

CORY. It looks like a stick.

GRANDMOTHER AUTUMN. It's a rose branch. It's going to grow back one day.

CORY. Is it sick?

GRANDMOTHER AUTUMN. Yes, it's been sick for a very long time.

CORY. Does it have a cold?

GRANDMOTHER AUTUMN. No.

CORY. Does it have a tummy ache?

GRANDMOTHER AUTUMN. No.

CORY. Does it have a toothache?

GRANDMOTHER AUTUMN. It's a plant. Plants don't get colds, tummy aches or toothaches.

CORY. Does it have a fever?

GRANDMOTHER AUTUMN. No.

CORY. Does it have a booboo?

GRANDMOTHER AUTUMN. No.

CORY. Maybe's it's sad.

GRANDMOTHER AUTUMN. Sad?

CORY. Sometimes when I get sick it's 'cause I'm sad.

GRANDMOTHER AUTUMN. My late husband planted it when your mommy was born. It bloomed beautiful roses for many, many years. I'd wear them in my hat to church. I miss those days.

CORY. I remember my mommy singing to me, combing my hair and giving me butterfly kisses before she went to heaven.

GRANDMOTHER AUTUMN. We lost your mommy to a sickness the doctors couldn't cure.

CORY. My *papi* taught mommy to be a cowgirl. They met at a rodeo. *Papi* was a bronc rider.

GRANDMOTHER AUTUMN. I never understood that attraction.

CORY. Huh?

GRANDMOTHER AUTUMN. Never mind.

(DOG comes up between them. GRANDMOTHER AUTUMN looks at him disdainfully. He backs away.)

GRANDMOTHER AUTUMN *(cont'd, to CORY)*. Remember what I told you. *(To DOG.)* Stay away from my rose plant.

(GRANDMOTHER AUTUMN exits.)

CORY. Boy, let's have some fun. We'll play "Tea and Biscuits!" It'll be you, Bandit and me. OK, you sit here. And I'll sit there. No, you sit here. And I'll sit there. No, you sit here. And I'll sit there. OK, you sit there and I'll sit here. No, you sit here and I'll sit there. Make up your mind, doggy! *(DOG grabs her toy dog, Bandit, and runs around with it. CORY chases after him.)* Hey, you can't do that! Give him back to me! *(DOG drops the toy dog and bites an itch. She picks up her toy with two fingers.)* Eew! Let's play "Jumping Bean," OK? Watch me!

Jump, jump, jumping bean,

Jump!

 (CORY jumps.)

Jump, jump, jumping bean,

Jump!

 (CORY jumps.)

Jump, jump, jumping bean,

Jump!

 (CORY jumps.)

Jump, jump, jumping bean,

 (DOG barks.)

Jump, jump, jumping bean.

 (DOG barks.)

Jump, jump, jumping bean,

 (DOG barks.)

Jump, jump, jumping bean …

 (DOG spins.)

Spin!

Jump, jump, jumping bean

Spin!

 (DOG spins and barks.)

Jump, jump, jumping bean

Spin!

 (DOG spins and barks.)

Jump, jump, jumping bean

Spin!

 (CORY and DOG spin. He barks.)

Jump, jump, jumping bean, fall!

 (They fall to the ground.)

You did it, boy! I'm a mess! Look at the clouds! That one looks like Deshana Puglese with pigtails. That one looks like a crocodile with spiky hair. Peace! That one … hmm … that one looks like a big booger! Do you know that d-o-g spelled backwards is g-o-d? Weird, huh?

GRANDMOTHER AUTUMN *(offstage)*. Cory, dinner's ready! Come wash your hands!

CORY. OK! *(To DOG.)* Stay.

(DOG runs off. GRANDMOTHER AUTUMN enters with a small plate and bowl. CORY sits down.)

CORY *(points)*. What's that?

GRANDMOTHER AUTUMN. Don't point. It's not polite. It's spinach.

CORY. Yuck!

GRANDMOTHER AUTUMN. And chicken soup.

CORY. Again?

GRANDMOTHER AUTUMN. That's all that's left. So eat. Try the spinach. You'll like it. Superheroes eat it.

CORY. They do?

GRANDMOTHER AUTUMN. You ever heard of Popeye the Sailor Man?

CORY. Nope.

GRANDMOTHER AUTUMN. He could open a can with his bare hands.

CORY. For reals?

GRANDMOTHER AUTUMN. For real.

CORY. I'm not very hungry.

GRANDMOTHER AUTUMN. You'll eat every bite. That's my rule.

(DOG pops his head in to look. CORY notices him, but GRANDMOTHER AUTUMN does not.)

CORY. May I have a glass of water please?

GRANDMOTHER AUTUMN. OK.

(CORY signals to him and DOG enters. CORY tries to spoon-feed him soup.)

CORY. Go!

(DOG exits as GRANDMOTHER AUTUMN enters with a glass of water.)

GRANDMOTHER AUTUMN. Oh, I see you're eating your chicken soup! I was right, wasn't I?

(CORY smiles and looks in the direction of DOG. GRAND-MOTHER AUTUMN sits down.)

CORY. May I have a napkin please?

GRANDMOTHER AUTUMN. I could have sworn I put one down. Never mind.

CORY. Thank you.

(GRANDMOTHER AUTUMN gets up and exits. CORY signals DOG back in. She holds the bowl out as DOG laps up the soup.)

CORY. Go!

(DOG exits. GRANDMOTHER AUTUMN enters with a napkin.)

GRANDMOTHER AUTUMN. My you're a messy eater. Here.

CORY. Thank you.

(GRANDMOTHER AUTUMN sits down again.)

CORY. May I have some Tabasco sauce?

GRANDMOTHER AUTUMN. Tabasco sauce? *(Suspicious.)* Fine. I'll get you Tabasco sauce.

(GRANDMOTHER AUTUMN gets up and exits as DOG runs in lapping up the soup.)

CORY. Go!

(DOG runs out but charges right back in for one more taste. He exits as GRANDMOTHER AUTUMN enters.)

GRANDMOTHER AUTUMN. Tabasco sauce.

CORY. No, I changed my mind. I'm all done! Bye!

(CORY walks out. GRANDMOTHER AUTUMN picks up the soup bowl and finds a dog hair.)

GRANDMOTHER AUTUMN. You again! How did you get in my house?

(DOG pops his head in and slurps. He is unseen by GRAND-MOTHER AUTUMN. She exits. The phone rings.)

GRANDMOTHER AUTUMN. Hello? Oh, it's you. I didn't expect you'd call. Cory's fine. It hasn't been easy. No thanks to you. What job? Construction? I can't imagine it. I received a letter from the bank. No, I haven't opened it. No, I'm not worried. Don't make any promises. I don't want to talk about it anymore. I'll get Cory. Cory!

CORY *(entering)*. Yes?

GRANDMOTHER AUTUMN. It's your daddy. He's on the phone. He wants to speak to you.

(CORY takes the phone.)

CORY. *Papi!?! Te estraño mucho. (I miss you a lot.)* When are you coming home? A month? It's a long time. *(Whispering.)* She's not very nice. She makes me eat chicken soup. She makes me go to church. I can't see a thing 'cause of those big hats. It's so boring! I found a dog. He likes to bring me things. He doesn't have a name yet. Can we keep him?

(GRANDMOTHER AUTUMN clears her throat.)

CORY *(cont'd)*. OK, bye, *Papi*! I love you! *¡Adios!*

GRANDMOTHER AUTUMN. Where are you sleeping? Is that safe? Who's worried? I'm not worried. Goodbye.

(GRANDMOTHER AUTUMN exits. Night. DOG enters whimpering. CORY follows. DOG carries a bow tie in his mouth.)

CORY *(whispering)*. Shhh, we have to be quiet, boy! We don't want Grandma to know. You can sleep here tonight. You're safe with me. What'd you bring me this time? *(He drops the bow tie.)* It's pretty. I'll keep that, too.

(CORY picks up GRANDMOTHER AUTUMN's church hat and puts it on.)

CORY *(cont'd)*. Oooh, look at me! I'm Esther the peacock! Oooh, I like to wear fancy church hats! Oooh, praise the Lord! *(She laughs. Imitating GRANDMOTHER AU-TUMN.)* Good morning, Sister Edwina! This is my grand-daughter Cory. I won't let her wear a cowboy hat in church 'cause the Lord hates cowgirls!

GRANDMOTHER AUTUMN *(offstage)*. Cory?

CORY. Sorry, Grandma! *(She puts the hat away and jumps onto the sofa bed. To DOG.)* OK, you lie there and I'll lie here. No, you lie there and I'll lie here. No, you lie there and I'll lie here. OK, you lie there and I'll lie here. Make up your mind, doggy! *(DOG crosses to GRANDMOTHER AUTUMN's hat.)* What are you doing? You're supposed to be in bed. *(DOG starts sniffing a hat. He sneezes all over CORY and the hat.)* Hey! *(DOG barks and bites into the hat.)* Oh, no! Give me that!

GRANDMOTHER AUTUMN *(offstage)*. What's going on?

(CORY grabs the hat, and DOG thinks it's a game.)

CORY. Let go!

GRANDMOTHER AUTUMN. Cory!

(CORY jumps into her sofa bed and DOG follows. She puts the blanket over him as GRANDMOTHER AUTUMN enters wearing a robe.)

GRANDMOTHER AUTUMN. What are you doing?

CORY. Nothing.

GRANDMOTHER AUTUMN. Go to bed!

CORY. OK!

(CORY throws the blanket over her head. GRANDMOTHER AUTUMN exits. Under the covers they struggle for the hat.)

CORY. Give it back! Let go!

GRANDMOTHER AUTUMN. Don't make me come in there!

CORY. You're gonna get us in trouble!

GRANDMOTHER AUTUMN. That's it!

CORY. Uh-oh!

(GRANDMOTHER AUTUMN enters. CORY sticks her head out of the blanket.)

GRANDMOTHER AUTUMN. Child, what is going on with you?

CORY. I can't sleep.

GRANDMOTHER AUTUMN. Why?

CORY. 'Cause … um …

GRANDMOTHER AUTUMN. I'm waiting.

CORY. 'Cause there's a monster under my bed.

GRANDMOTHER AUTUMN. I told you there are no monsters.

CORY. Something's down there. I don't know.

GRANDMOTHER AUTUMN. I am not going to look.

CORY. Can I sleep in your bed?

GRANDMOTHER AUTUMN. Fine, I'll look.

(GRANDMOTHER AUTUMN bends down and begins to crawl under the sofa bed. It's a tight space for her.)

GRANDMOTHER AUTUMN *(cont'd, struggling)*. I see no monsters!

(CORY lifts up the blanket and tries to pull the hat away from DOG.)

CORY. Let go!

GRANDMOTHER AUTUMN. Hey, what's my letter doing under here? Was it that dog!?!

(CORY and DOG pull at GRANDMOTHER AUTUMN's hat.)

CORY. Give it here! *(DOG growls.)* Let go! Aaggghhh!

(The hat is destroyed. GRANDMOTHER AUTUMN crawls out from under the sofa bed.)

GRANDMOTHER AUTUMN. That's my hat!

(DOG shakes the hat playfully in his mouth.)

CORY. I'm sorry!

GRANDMOTHER AUTUMN. It's ruined!

CORY. I can fix it!

GRANDMOTHER AUTUMN *(to DOG)*. Get out of here!

CORY. No!

GRANDMOTHER AUTUMN. GET!

(DOG exits. CORY runs out. GRANDMOTHER AUTUMN holds out the letter.)

GRANDMOTHER AUTUMN *(cont'd)*. Oh, Lord. They're going to take my house.

(She exits. DOG re-enters, retrieves the hat and exits. The phone rings. CORY and GRANDMOTHER AUTUMN enter answering the phone call.)

CORY *(crying)*. *Papi*, she sent him away.

GRANDMOTHER AUTUMN. I'm doing everything I can.

CORY. He's my only friend.

GRANDMOTHER AUTUMN. I've got till the end of the month to pay or I lose my home.

CORY. Make it up to her? How?

GRANDMOTHER AUTUMN. I'm at my wits end.

CORY. I'm being a good girl.

GRANDMOTHER AUTUMN. Please don't make any promises. You live in a truck.

CORY. OK, *sí*, OK. I'll try harder, *sí*!

(They hang up.)

CORY. I promise to eat your chicken soup and like it.

GRANDMOTHER AUTUMN. What?

CORY. I know that you hate *Papi* and me.

GRANDMOTHER AUTUMN. How can you think that?

CORY. You never talk nice to us and you're always in a bad way.

GRANDMOTHER AUTUMN. Well, I'm sorry. I have a lot on my mind and my tooth hurts.

CORY. Did you love my mommy?

GRANDMOTHER AUTUMN. Yes, I did. Very much. I don't hate you, OK?

CORY. OK.

GRANDMOTHER AUTUMN. You were right, you know?

CORY. About what?

GRANDMOTHER AUTUM. At church when I bent the truth about visiting you. I never did. I wasn't very understanding of your mommy and daddy's love for one another. I didn't talk to her until it was too late when she was sick, and I'm truly sorry for that. Truly sorry.

CORY. My mommy told me that the butterfly kisses she liked to give me she learned from you.

GRANDMOTHER AUTUMN. She did?

CORY. Yup. You taught her that?

GRANDMOTHER AUTUMN. Ah huh.

(They exit. Time has passed. CORY enters wearing a cape, goggles and cowboy hat.)

CORY. Hey, boy, you're back! I missed you! *(DOG enters carrying a plastic rose flower. He drops it in front of CORY.)* You brought me a plastic flower. You wanna play superheroes? *(He barks.)* My *papi* helped me make my own cape! See! Now, you need one! Where can I—I know! *(CORY crosses to the covered rose bush and removes the plastic.)* This will do! Don't move! *(She places the plastic bag on him.)* Yeehaw, it's Super Cowgirl and Mighty Dog! We can fly fast, jump high and we're super strong! *(CORY runs around the yard as if she is flying. DOG follows. She stops and points.)* Oh, look, Mighty Dog, there's a little old lady who needs our help! Those wild dogs are gonna tear her to pieces! Let's use our super x-ray vision to stop them! *(She makes "buzzing" sound. DOG barks.)* It's no good! They got deflectors! It's time for super kung-fu! Let's kick butt! *(Kicking and karate chopping. DOG runs around barking.)* Hiya! Hiya! Hiya! We did it Mighty Dog! We saved the little old lady! *(DOG chews on the plastic.)* Hey, stop chewing your cape! You'll lose your super powers! *(DOG runs around barking and exits. To imaginary little old lady.)* Don't cry, ma'am. No need for tears. Yes, I would love an ice cream cone with sprinkles! *Muchas gracias. (DOG enters carrying GRANDMOTHER AUTUMN's hat. He drops it in front of CORY.)* Hey, that's Grandma's hat. *(She picks up the hat and places it with the flower, side by side.)* That looks real pretty together. Hey, I bet if we add the other stuff you brought me Grandma would really like it! *(To DOG.)* You did it, Mighty Dog!

GRANDMOTHER AUTUMN *(offstage)*. Cory?

CORY. You gotta go! *(DOG sits.)* Why don't you ever do what I say?

GRANDMOTHER AUTUMN *(offstage)*. Where are you?

(DOG exits as GRANDMOTHER AUTUMN enters.)

CORY. I'm out here all alone, Grandma.

GRANDMOTHER AUTUMN. You're supposed to keep the front gate closed. That's my rule remember?

CORY. Oh, yeah, I forgot. *(Holding out the church hat.)* Look!

GRANDMOTHER AUTUMN. Is that my church hat?

CORY. Yup!

GRANDMOTHER AUTUMN. It looks different.

CORY. I think it's real pretty.

GRANDMOTHER AUTUMN. You did this?

CORY. The Lord works in mysterious ways.

(GRANDMOTHER AUTUMN takes the hat from CORY.)

GRANDMOTHER AUTUMN. I'll say. With a little cleaning, sewing and rearranging—

CORY *(holding up a feather)*. And a big feather! It'll look like new!

GRANDMOTHER AUTUMN. We'll see about that.

(GRANDMOTHER AUTUMN and CORY exit. DOG enters, takes the rose shoot and exits. The phone rings. GRANDMOTHER AUTUMN and CORY pick up.)

GRANDMOTHER AUTUMN. Hello?

CORY. *Papi!*

GRANDMOTHER AUTUMN. She's fine.

CORY. I can't wait to see you.

GRANDMOTHER AUTUMN. What?

CORY. What time will you be here?

GRANDMOTHER AUTUMN. Overtime?

CORY. You're coming later?

GRANDMOTHER AUTUMN. You know that child has been expecting you all month.

CORY. You're not coming?

GRANDMOTHER AUTUMN. I'll think of something.

CORY. OK, OK, *sí, sí.*

GRANDMOTHER AUTUMN. Your *papi* is working real hard. I know it saddens him to be away from you, but it's only for a little while. He doesn't want you to live in a shelter or sleep in a truck anymore. He promised he'd write.

CORY. For reals?

GRANDMOTHER AUTUMN. For real.

(Time passes. Music. GRANDMOTHER AUTUMN enters gently brushing her teeth. She stands before an imaginary sink and mirror. CORY gets up and brushes her teeth before an imaginary sink and mirror. They go through their morning ritual unaware of what the other is doing. GRANDMOTHER AUTUMN puts on her church hat. It is now smaller but more beautiful. CORY puts on her cowboy hat.)

CORY. Yeehaw, Super Cowgirl!

GRANDMOTHER AUTUMN. You can't wear that in church.

CORY. But I spoke to the Lord and he said it was "OK."

GRANDMOTHER AUTUMN. The Lord didn't speak to me about it. *(She takes the cowboy hat off CORY. GRANDMOTHER AUTUMN carries her umbrella.)* Let's hurry!

(Church music. GRANDMOTHER AUTUMN and CORY sit.)

GRANDMOTHER AUTUMN *(to the unseen church ladies)*. Sister Edwina, Hattie, Esther. Oh, this? I made it myself … Saw it in a magazine from … Atlanta!

CORY. Huh?

GRANDMOTHER AUTUMN *(to CORY)*. Close your mouth! *(To the unseen church ladies.)* It's what's called "vintage." It's the new thing these days. Ladies.

CORY *(whispering)*. You lied again.

GRANDMOTHER AUTUMN *(whispering)*. You're right. *(To the unseen church ladies.)* Truthfully, Ladies, I didn't see it in a magazine. It's my old hat that I—We recycled into something new. Well, it does look new, doesn't it?

(Church music is heard. GRANDMOTHER AUTUMN joins in with the congregation. DOG enters. In his mouth is the rose shoot. He drops it in front of GRANDMOTHER AUTUMN and CORY.)

GRANDMOTHER AUTUMN. My rose plant! I'm going to kill that dog!

(DOG yelps and exits.)

CORY. No!

(GRANDMOTHER AUTUMN chases after DOG. CORY follows. GRANDMOTHER AUTUMN enters with DOG on a leash. She secures it so he can't escape.)

GRANDMOTHER AUTUMN. This dog is going to the pound!

CORY. What's that mean?

GRANDMOTHER AUTUMN. That's where bad dogs go.

CORY. If he goes, I go, too! Woof! Woof!

GRANDMOTHER AUTUMN. Stop it!

CORY. Woof! Woof!

GRANDMOTHER AUTUMN. Bad dogs go to the pound and they never come back!

CORY. No, you can't do that!

GRANDMOTHER AUTUMN. Now close that gate!

(GRANDMOTHER AUTUMN exits.)

CORY. I won't let her take you to the pound. You're my best friend. We're gonna have to go far away, OK? *(She unties the leash. DOG becomes alert.)* What is it, boy? *(DOG growls as a pack of wild dogs approach.)* Oh, no! Grandma! *(DOG steps in front of CORY, confronting the wild dogs.)* GRANDMA!

(Fierce barking is heard as DOG fights them while CORY pulls his leash back. GRANDMOTHER AUTUMN enters with a broom, beating them back.)

GRANDMOTHER AUTUMN. Get! Get! GET!

(DOG is lying on the ground.)

CORY. He's hurt real bad!

GRANDMOTHER AUTUMN. Don't touch him!

CORY. Grandma, do something!

GRANDMOTHER AUTUMN. We're taking Mr. Johnson's car!

CORY. You saved me, boy. He saved me.

GRANDMOTHER AUTUMN. Get in!

(Sound of car starting up.)

CORY *(to DOG)*. It's gonna be OK, boy!

GRANDMOTHER AUTUMN. Put your seatbelt on!

CORY. You're my best friend.

GRANDMOTHER AUTUMN. Where's the clutch?

CORY. Grandma, do you know how to drive?

GRANDMOTHER AUTUMN. Here goes nothing!

(GRANDMOTHER AUTUMN floors the gas pedal.)

CORY. Look out for Sister Esther!

GRANDMOTHER AUTUMN. Get out of the way! Sorry!

CORY. I should've kept the gate closed!

GRANDMOTHER AUTUMN. It's not your fault.

CORY. I should've remembered your rule!

GRANDMOTHER AUTUMN. You're not to blame.

CORY. Stupid girl!

GRANDMOTHER AUTUMN. No, you're not a stupid girl!
(Car screeches to a stop. Speaking to the unseen veterinarian.) Can you save him, Doctor?

CORY. He's gonna fix you up, boy!

GRANDMOTHER AUTUMN. What two options?

CORY. Good as new!

GRANDMOTHER AUTUMN. How much?

CORY .We'll play together again!

GRANDMOTHER AUTUMN. No, I don't want him put down!

CORY. Grandma!

GRANDMOTHER AUTUMN. I don't care how much it costs! Take my wedding ring!

CORY. He's not breathing!

GRANDMOTHER AUTUMN. He saved my grandbaby!

CORY. He's not breathing!

GRANDMOTHER AUTUMN. Please we need a miracle!

(They exit. A few days later. CORY re-enters. She wears her cowboy hat. GRANDMOTHER AUTUMN wears her church hat.)

GRANDMOTHER AUTUMN. Shall we begin?

CORY. OK. *(She digs a hole in the ground.)*

GRANDMOTHER AUTUMN. Bow your head. We return this mighty gift back from whence it came. Thank you for its many blessings—

(CORY holds up the rose shoot.)

GRANDMOTHER AUTUMN *(cont'd)*. —and for giving us a second chance. *(She buries it.)*

CORY. Amen.

GRANDMOTHER AUTUMN. I've been angry and feeling sorry for myself and I blamed everyone. You're the best thing in my life, a real Super Cowgirl.

CORY. Me?

GRANDMOTHER AUTUMN. You never gave up on us. *(Beat.)* You remind me of your mommy.

CORY. I do?

GRANDMOTHER AUTUMN. She had a beautiful smile like you, such an imagination, and she always wanted a dog. That's why I gave her Bandit.

(GRANDMOTHER AUTUMN hands CORY her toy dog.)

CORY. You gave him to her?

GRANDMOTHER AUTUMN. Yes.

CORY. And now he's mine.

(CORY hugs her toy dog. DOG enters wearing a sling on his arm.)

CORY. Hey, boy!

(CORY places her toy dog away and crosses to DOG.)

GRANDMOTHER AUTUMN. You pick a name for him yet?

CORY. Nope.

GRANDMOTHER AUTUMN. I think you should name him "Wimpy." *(She imitates DOG.)* Oh, I forgot! I've got something for you.

CORY. Is it a monkey?

GRANDMOTHER AUTUMN. What? No.

CORY. Is it a rhino on a skateboard?

GRANDMOTHER AUTUMN. No, but I see what you're doing.

CORY. Is it a duck with glasses?

GRANDMOTHER AUTUMN. No.

CORY. Is it a—

GRANDMOTHER AUTUMN. Here!

(GRANDMOTHER AUTUMN gives CORY an envelope.)

CORY. It's from *Papi*!

GRANDMOTHER AUTUMN. What's he say?

(CORY rips opens the envelope, removing the letter. DOG discovers the envelope on the ground.)

CORY. He drew me a picture with words. *Papi's* wearing cowboy boots, hat and riding in a rodeo! I'm there too! Look, that's you.

GRANDMOTHER AUTUMN. He drew me into the picture?

CORY. That's 'cause you're family.

GRANDMOTHER AUTUMN. He told you that?

CORY. Yup. He said that you brought Mommy into the world and that was pretty special 'cause he would have never met Mommy and I'd never been born. *(Taking the envelope from DOG.)* Look!

GRANDMOTHER AUTUMN. What is it?

CORY. Money.

(CORY hands it to GRANDMOTHER AUTUMN.)

GRANDMOTHER AUTUMN. I didn't expect this …

CORY. Are you crying?

GRANDMOTHER AUTUMN. I'm not crying.

CORY. Are we going to have to live in a truck again?

GRANDMOTHER AUTUMN. Don't you worry none. We're going to manage. With what your *papi* sent and with what the church ladies are willing to pay me—

CORY. Pay you for what?

GRANDMOTHER AUTUMN. Child, they liked my vintage hat so much that they're going to pay me to redo all of theirs. Our church has a lot of old ladies with a lot of old hats! We're gonna be busy. Super Cowgirls!

CORY. Yeehaw!

(DOG runs up to GRANDMOTHER AUTUMN.)

GRANDMOTHER AUTUMN. Dog, you need a bath.

CORY. I know what to name him now!

GRANDMOTHER AUTUMN. What?

CORY. Miracle!

GRANDMOTHER AUTUMN. Miracle?

GRANDMOTHER AUTUMN & CORY *(proudly)*. Mighty Miracle!

(MIRACLE barks.)

END OF PLAY

NOTES

NOTES

NOTES

NOTES

NOTES

NOTES